I0428275

September 2013

FEDERAL INFORMATION SECURITY

Mixed Progress in Implementing Program Components; Improved Metrics Needed to Measure Effectiveness

FEDERAL INFORMATION SECURITY

Mixed Progress in Implementing Program Components; Improved Metrics Needed to Measure Effectiveness

GAO

Highlights

Highlights of GAO-13-776, a report to congressional committees

Why GAO Did This Study

FISMA requires the Comptroller General to periodically report to Congress on agency implementation of the act's provisions. To this end, this report summarizes GAO's evaluation of the extent to which agencies have implemented the requirements of FISMA, including the adequacy and effectiveness of agency information security policies and practices. To do this, GAO analyzed its previous information security reports, annual FISMA reports and other reports from the 24 major federal agencies, reports from inspectors general, and OMB's annual reports to Congress on FISMA implementation. GAO also interviewed agency officials at OMB, DHS, NIST, and 6 agencies selected using the total number of systems the agencies reported in fiscal year 2011.

What GAO Recommends

GAO and inspectors general have previously made numerous recommendations to improve agencies' information security programs. The agencies generally agreed with GAO's recommendations. In addition, GAO previously recommended that OMB revise annual reporting guidance to require performance targets to which OMB generally agreed. GAO is also recommending that the Director of OMB ensure that metrics are incorporated that assess the effectiveness of information security programs in OMB's annual FISMA reporting instructions to agencies and inspectors general.

View GAO-13-776. For more information, contact Gregory C. Wilshusen at (202) 512-6244 or wilshuseng@gao.gov.

What GAO Found

In fiscal year 2012, 24 major federal agencies had established many of the components of an information security program required by The Federal Information Security Management Act of 2002 (FISMA); however, they had partially established others. FISMA requires each federal agency to establish an information security program that incorporates eight key components, and each agency inspector general to annually evaluate and report on the information security program and practices of the agency. The act also requires the Office of Management and Budget (OMB) to develop and oversee the implementation of policies, principles, standards, and guidelines on information security in federal agencies and the National Institute of Standards and Technology to develop security standards and guidelines. The table below shows agency implementation of information security program components in fiscal year 2012.

Agency Implementation of Information Security Program Components in Fiscal Year 2012

Program components	Number of agencies	
	Fully implemented	Partially implemented
Establishing a program for managing information security risk	18	6
Documenting policies and procedures	10	12[a]
Selecting security controls for systems	18	6
Establishing a security training program	22	2
Monitoring controls on an ongoing basis	13	10[b]
Establishing a remediation program	19	5
Establishing an incident response and reporting program	20	3[b]
Establishing a continuity of operations program	18	5[b]

Source: GAO analysis of agency and inspector general data.

[a]An additional two agencies did not fully evaluate this program component in fiscal year 2012.

[b]One additional agency did not fully evaluate this program component in fiscal year 2012.

The extent to which agencies implemented security program components showed mixed progress from fiscal year 2011 to fiscal year 2012. For example, according to inspectors general reports, the number of agencies that had analyzed, validated, and documented security incidents increased from 16 to 19, while the number able to track identified weaknesses declined from 20 to 15. GAO and inspectors general continue to identify weaknesses in elements of agencies' programs, such as the implementation of specific security controls. For instance, in fiscal year 2012, almost all (23 of 24) of the major federal agencies had weaknesses in the controls that are intended to limit or detect access to computer resources.

OMB and the Department of Homeland Security (DHS) continued to develop reporting metrics and assist agencies in improving their information security programs; however, the metrics do not evaluate all FISMA requirements, such as conducting risk assessments and developing security plans; are focused mainly on compliance rather than effectiveness of controls; and in many cases did not identify specific performance targets for determining levels of implementation. Enhancements to these metrics would provide additional insight into agency information security programs.

_____ **United States Government Accountability Office**

Contents

Figures

GAO
U.S. GOVERNMENT ACCOUNTABILITY OFFICE

441 G St. N.W.
Washington, DC 20548

September 26, 2013

The Honorable Thomas R. Carper
Chairman
The Honorable Tom Coburn, M.D.
Ranking Member
Committee on Homeland Security and Governmental Affairs
United States Senate

The Honorable Darrell E. Issa
Chairman
The Honorable Elijah E. Cummings
Ranking Member
Committee on Oversight and Government Reform
House of Representatives

The pervasive use of the Internet has revolutionized the way that our government, our nation, and the rest of the world communicate and conduct business. While the benefits have been enormous, this widespread connectivity also poses significant risks to the government's and our nation's computer systems and networks as well as to the critical operations and key infrastructures they support. The speed and accessibility that create the benefits of the computer age, if not properly controlled, can allow unauthorized individuals and organizations to inexpensively eavesdrop on or interfere with these operations from remote locations for potentially malicious purposes, including fraud or sabotage.

Increasingly sophisticated cyber threats have underscored the need to manage and bolster the cybersecurity of key government systems as well as the nation's critical infrastructure.[1] For example, advanced persistent threats—where an adversary that possesses sophisticated levels of expertise and significant resources can attack using multiple means such

---

[1]Critical infrastructure includes systems and assets so vital to the United States that their incapacity or destruction would have a debilitating impact on national security. These critical infrastructures are chemical; commercial facilities; communications; critical manufacturing; dams; defense industrial base; emergency services; energy; financial services; food and agriculture; government facilities; healthcare and public health; information technology; nuclear reactors, materials, and waste; transportation systems; and water and wastewater systems.

as cyber, physical, or deception to achieve its objectives—pose increasing risks.

The security of our computer networks and systems, including federal information systems, continues to be an issue of pressing concern for the nation. The President has declared the cyber threat to be "[o]ne of the most serious economic and national security challenges we face as a nation" and stated that "America's economic prosperity in the 21st century will depend on cybersecurity."[2] On October 11, 2012, the Secretary of Defense stated that the collective result of attacks on our nation's critical infrastructure could be "a cyber Pearl Harbor; an attack that would cause physical destruction and the loss of life."[3] To further highlight the importance of the threat, the Director of National Intelligence has also warned of the increasing globalization of cyber attacks. In March 2013, he testified that cyber threats are growing more interconnected and viral and that we can now include cyber on the list of weapons being used against the United States.[4] These growing and evolving threats can potentially affect all segments of our society, including individuals, private businesses, government agencies, and other entities.

We have identified the protection of federal information systems as a government-wide high-risk area since 1997 and, in 2003 expanded this high-risk area to include the protection of systems supporting the nation's critical infrastructures.[5] Since that time, we have issued numerous reports making recommendations to address weaknesses in federal information security programs. We continued to identify this area as high risk in February 2013 based on the (1) increasing dependence of the federal government and our nation's critical infrastructures on computerized information systems and electronic data to carry out operations and to process, maintain, and report essential information; (2) increasing prevalence and sophistication of cyber threats and incidents affecting

---

[2]President Barack Obama, "Remarks by the President on Securing Our Nation's Cyber Infrastructure" (Washington, D.C.: May 29, 2009).

[3]Secretary of Defense Leon E. Panetta, "Remarks by Secretary Panetta on Cybersecurity to the Business Executives for National Security, New York City" (New York, N.Y.: Oct. 11, 2012).

[4]James R. Clapper, Director of National Intelligence, "Worldwide Threat Assessment to the Senate Select Committee on Intelligence" (Mar. 12, 2013).

[5]See GAO, *High Risk Series: An Overview*, GAO/HR-97-1 (Washington, D.C.: February 1997), and *High Risk Series: An Update*, GAO-03-119 (Washington, D.C.: January 2003).

those information systems and data; and (3) continuing challenges faced by the federal government to effectively implement cybersecurity.[6]

The Federal Information Security Management Act of 2002 (FISMA)[7] established information security program and evaluation requirements for federal agencies. In addition, FISMA also assigns specific responsibilities to the Office of Management and Budget (OMB) and the National Institute of Standards and Technology (NIST). Each agency and its office of inspector general are to report annually to OMB, selected congressional committees, and the Comptroller General on the adequacy of its information security policies, procedures, practices, and compliance with requirements. The act also requires the Comptroller General to periodically report to Congress on agency implementation of the act's provisions.

Our objective was to evaluate the extent to which major federal agencies have implemented the requirements of FISMA, including the adequacy and effectiveness of agency information security policies and practices. To accomplish this for fiscal years 2011 and 2012, we analyzed our previous information security reports, annual agency FISMA reports, and agency financial and performance and accountability reports from the 24 major federal agencies covered by the Chief Financial Officers Act,[8] reports from the 24 agencies' offices of inspector general, OMB's annual reports to Congress on FISMA implementation, and NIST security publications. Where possible, we categorized findings from those reports according to information security program requirements prescribed by FISMA and security control areas defined by our Federal Information System Controls Audit Manual.[9] We also conducted interviews with

---

[6] GAO, *High-Risk Series: An Update*, GAO-13-283 (Washington, D.C.: February 2013).

[7] Pub. L. No. 107-347, Title III, 116 Stat. 2899, 2946 (Dec. 17, 2002).

[8] The 24 major departments and agencies are the Departments of Agriculture, Commerce, Defense, Education, Energy, Health and Human Services, Homeland Security, Housing and Urban Development, the Interior, Justice, Labor, State, Transportation, the Treasury, and Veterans Affairs; the Environmental Protection Agency, General Services Administration, National Aeronautics and Space Administration, National Science Foundation, Nuclear Regulatory Commission, Office of Personnel Management, Small Business Administration, Social Security Administration, and U.S. Agency for International Development.

[9] GAO, *Federal Information System Controls Audit Manual (FISCAM)*, GAO-09-232G (Washington, D.C.: February 2009).

agency officials at OMB, the Department of Homeland Security (DHS), NIST, and 6 selected agencies. For the 6 agencies, we collected data from inspectors general and agency officials to ensure the reliability of agency data submissions. Based on this assessment, we determined that the data were sufficiently reliable for our work.

We conducted this performance audit from February 2013 to September 2013 in accordance with generally accepted government auditing standards. Those standards require that we plan and perform the audit to obtain sufficient, appropriate evidence to provide a reasonable basis for our findings and conclusions based on our audit objectives. We believe that the evidence obtained provides a reasonable basis for our findings and conclusions based on our audit objectives. For more details on our objective, scope, and methodology, see appendix I.

Background

To help protect against threats to federal systems, FISMA sets forth a comprehensive framework for ensuring the effectiveness of information security controls over information resources that support federal operations and assets. This framework creates a cycle of risk management activities necessary for an effective security program. It is also intended to provide a mechanism for improved oversight of federal agency information security programs.

To ensure the implementation of this framework, FISMA assigns specific responsibilities to agencies, their inspectors general, OMB, and NIST.

FISMA requires each agency to develop, document, and implement an information security program that includes the following components:

- periodic assessments of the risk and magnitude of harm that could result from the unauthorized access, use, disclosure, disruption, modification, or destruction of information or information systems;

- policies and procedures that (1) are based on risk assessments, (2) cost-effectively reduce information security risks to an acceptable level, (3) ensure that information security is addressed throughout the life cycle of each system, and (4) ensure compliance with applicable requirements;

- subordinate plans for providing adequate information security for networks, facilities, and systems or group of information systems, as appropriate;

- security awareness training to inform personnel of information security risks and of their responsibilities in complying with agency policies and procedures, as well as training personnel with significant security responsibilities for information security;

- periodic testing and evaluation of the effectiveness of information security policies, procedures, and practices, to be performed with a frequency depending on risk, but no less than annually, and that includes testing of management, operational, and technical controls for every system identified in the agency's required inventory of major information systems;

- a process for planning, implementing, evaluating, and documenting remedial action to address any deficiencies in the information security policies, procedures, and practices of the agency;

- procedures for detecting, reporting, and responding to security incidents; and

- plans and procedures to ensure continuity of operations for information systems that support the operations and assets of the agency.

In addition, agencies are to report annually to OMB, certain congressional committees, and the Comptroller General on the adequacy and effectiveness of information security policies, procedures, and practices, and compliance with FISMA. The act also requires each agency inspector general, or other independent auditor, to annually evaluate and report on the information security program and practices of the agency.

OMB's responsibilities include developing and overseeing the implementation of policies, principles, standards, and guidelines on information security in federal agencies (except with regard to national security systems[10]). It is also responsible for ensuring the operation of a

---

[10]As defined in FISMA, the term "national security system" means any information system used by or on behalf of a federal agency that (1) involves intelligence activities, national security-related cryptologic activities, command and control of military forces, or equipment that is an integral part of a weapon or weapons system, or is critical to the direct fulfillment of military or intelligence missions (excluding systems used for routine administrative and business applications); or (2) is protected at all times by procedures established for handling classified national security information. See 44 U.S.C. § 3542(b)(2).

federal information security incident center. The required functions of this center are performed by the DHS United States Computer Emergency Readiness Team (US-CERT), which was established to aggregate and disseminate cybersecurity information to improve warning and response to incidents, increase coordination of response information, reduce vulnerabilities, and enhance prevention and protection. OMB is also responsible for reviewing, at least annually, and approving or disapproving agency information security programs.

Since it began issuing guidance to agencies in 2003, OMB has instructed agency chief information officers and inspectors general to report on a variety of metrics in order to satisfy reporting requirements established by FISMA. Over time, these metrics have evolved to include administration priorities and baseline metrics meant to allow for measurement of agency progress in implementing information security-related priorities and controls. OMB requires agencies and inspectors general to use an interactive data collection tool called CyberScope[11] to respond to these metrics. The metrics are used by OMB to summarize agencies' progress in meeting FISMA requirements and report this progress to Congress in an annual report as required by FISMA.

NIST's responsibilities under FISMA include the development of security standards and guidelines for agencies that include standards for categorizing information and information systems according to ranges of risk levels, minimum security requirements for information and information systems in risk categories, guidelines for detection and handling of information security incidents, and guidelines for identifying an information system as a national security system. (See app. II for additional information on agency responsibilities under FISMA.)

In the 11 years since FISMA was enacted into law, executive branch oversight of agency information security has changed. As part of its FISMA oversight responsibilities, OMB has issued annual instructions for agencies and inspectors general to meet FISMA reporting requirements. However, in July 2010, the Director of OMB and the White House

---

[11]CyberScope is an interactive data collection tool that has the capability to receive data feeds on a recurring basis to assess the security posture of a federal agency's information infrastructure. Agencies are required to use this tool to respond to reporting metrics.

Cybersecurity Coordinator issued a joint memorandum[12] stating that DHS was to exercise primary responsibility within the executive branch for the operational aspects of cybersecurity for federal information systems that fall within the scope of FISMA. The memo stated that DHS activities would include five specific responsibilities of OMB under FISMA:

- overseeing implementation of and reporting on government cybersecurity policies and guidance;
- overseeing and assisting government efforts to provide adequate, risk-based, and cost-effective cybersecurity;
- overseeing agencies' compliance with FISMA;
- overseeing agencies' cybersecurity operations and incident response; and
- annually reviewing agencies' cybersecurity programs.

The OMB memo also stated that in carrying out these responsibilities, DHS is to be subject to general OMB oversight in accordance with the provisions of FISMA. In addition, the memo stated that the Cybersecurity Coordinator would lead the interagency process for cybersecurity strategy and policy development. Subsequent to the issuance of this memo, both OMB and DHS began issuing annual reporting instructions to agencies[13] and DHS began issuing reporting metrics to agencies and inspectors general instead of OMB.

Within DHS, the Federal Network Resilience division's Cybersecurity Performance Management Branch is responsible for (1) developing and disseminating FISMA reporting metrics, (2) managing the CyberScope web-based application, and (3) collecting and reviewing federal agencies' cybersecurity data submissions and monthly data feeds to CyberScope. In addition, the Cybersecurity Assurance Program Branch is responsible for conducting cybersecurity reviews and assessments at federal agencies to evaluate the effectiveness of agencies' information security programs.

---

[12]OMB, Memorandum M-10-28, *Clarifying Cybersecurity Responsibilities and Activities of the Executive Office of the President and the Department of Homeland Security* (Washington, D.C.: July 6, 2010).

[13]Fiscal year 2011 reporting instructions for FISMA and agency privacy management were issued by DHS, as Federal Information Security Memorandum 11-02 (Aug. 24, 2011), and by OMB, as M-11-33 (Sept. 14, 2011). Fiscal year 2012 reporting instructions were issued by DHS, as Federal Information Security Memorandum 12-02 (Feb. 15, 2012), and by OMB, as M-12-20 (Sept. 27, 2012). While identically titled, these memos varied in content.

Mixed Progress Has Been Made in Implementing Many FISMA Requirements, but Weaknesses Continue in Agencies' Security Programs

In fiscal year 2012, agencies and their inspectors general reported mixed progress from fiscal year 2011 in implementing many of the requirements for establishing an entity-wide information security program. According to inspectors general reports, agencies (1) improved in establishing a program for managing information security risk; (2) generally documented information security program policies and procedures; (3) generally implemented certain elements of security planning; (4) declined in providing security awareness training but improved in providing specialized training; (5) generally established test and evaluation programs and are working toward establishing continuous monitoring programs; (6) declined in implementing elements of a remediation program; (7) generally established programs for detecting, responding to, and reporting security incidents; and (8) declined in implementing elements of continuity of operations programs. Notwithstanding the mixed progress made, GAO and inspectors general continue to identify weaknesses in agencies' information security programs and make recommendations to mitigate the weaknesses identified. In addition, OMB and DHS continued to develop reporting metrics and assist agencies in improving their information security programs; however, the metrics do not evaluate all FISMA requirements, focused mainly on compliance rather than effectiveness of controls, and in many cases did not identify specific performance targets for determining levels of implementation. Finally, inspectors general conducted the required independent evaluations of agency information security programs, and NIST continued to issue guidance to assist agencies with implementing controls to improve their information security posture.

An Increasing Number of Agencies Have Implemented Programs for Managing Information Security Risk, but Weaknesses Remain in Program Elements

FISMA requires that the head of each agency provide information security protections commensurate with the risk resulting from unauthorized access, use, disclosure, disruption, modification, or destruction of agency information and information systems. FISMA specifically requires agencies to assess this risk in order to determine the appropriate controls needed to remediate or mitigate the risk to the agency. To assist agencies in identifying risks, NIST has issued risk management and assessment guides for organizations and information systems.[14] According to NIST's Guide for Applying the Risk Management Framework to Federal Information Systems, risk management is addressed at the organization level, the mission and business process level, and the information system level. Risks are addressed from an organizational perspective with the development of, among other things, risk management policies, procedures, and strategy. The risk decisions made at the organizational level guide the entire risk management program.

Agencies made progress in implementing programs for managing information security risk in fiscal year 2012. According to inspectors general reports, an increasing number of agencies implemented a program for managing information security risk that is consistent with FISMA requirements and its implementing guidance. Specifically, 18 of 24 agencies in fiscal year 2012 implemented such a program compared to 8 of 24 in 2011. In addition, an increasing number of agencies documented policies, procedures, and strategies—three key components for assessing and managing risk. Figure 1 shows agency progress in documenting and implementing a risk management program and key elements of that program in fiscal years 2011 and 2012.

---

[14]NIST, *Managing Information Security Risk: Organization, Mission, and Information System View,* NIST Special Publication 800-39 (Gaithersburg, Md.: March 2011); *Guide for Applying the Risk Management Framework to Federal Information Systems: A Security Life Cycle Approach*, NIST Special Publication 800-37 Revision 1 (Gaithersburg, Md.: February 2010); and *Guide for Conducting Risk Assessments*, NIST Special Publication 800-30 Revision 1 (Gaithersburg, Md.: September 2012).

Figure 1: Number of the 24 Major Agencies Documenting and Implementing Risk Management Programs and Key Elements of that Program in Fiscal Years 2011 and 2012

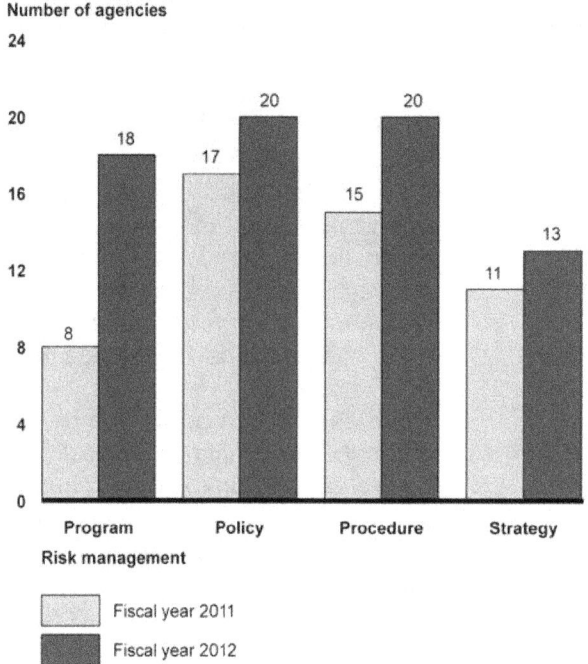

Source: GAO analysis of inspectors general FISMA reports for fiscal years 2011 and 2012.

Although an increasing number of agencies have implemented a risk management program and documented policies, procedures, and strategies, agency inspectors general identified areas for improvement in their agency's risk assessment and management activities. For example, in fiscal year 2012, 20 of 24 agencies had weaknesses in periodically assessing and validating risks. To illustrate, 1 agency did not conduct a risk assessment to ensure that the impact of mobile devices and their associated vulnerabilities were adequately addressed. Another agency's risk assessments were not properly updated, as they included references to inaccurate system environment information. Another agency was missing key elements in its approach to managing risk at an agency-wide level, including conducting an agency-wide risk assessment and communicating risks to system owners. In addition, fewer agencies addressed risk from a mission or business perspective in fiscal year 2012 than in fiscal year 2011, declining from 15 to 14 agencies. Risk management is at the center of an effective information security program, and without an effective risk management program agencies may not be fully aware of the risks to essential computing resources, and may not be able to make informed decisions about needed security protections.

Most Agencies Documented Information Security Program Policies and Procedures, but Implementation Was Inconsistent

FISMA requires agencies to develop, document, and implement policies and procedures that

- are based on risk assessments;
- cost-effectively reduce information security risks to an acceptable level;
- ensure that information security is addressed throughout the life cycle of each agency information system; and
- ensure compliance with FISMA requirements, OMB policies and procedures, minimally acceptable system configuration requirements, and any other applicable requirements.

In fiscal years 2011 and 2012, OMB asked inspectors general to report on whether agencies had documented policies and procedures for 11 information system control categories.[15] These controls are intended to (1) manage risks to organizational operations, assets, and individuals resulting from the operation of information systems; (2) provide reasonable assurance that changes to information system resources are authorized and systems are configured and operating securely and as intended; (3) rapidly detect incidents, minimize loss and destruction, mitigate exploited weaknesses, and restore IT services; (4) inform agency personnel of the information security risks associated with their activities and inform agency personnel of their responsibilities in complying with agency policies and procedures designed to reduce these risks; (5) ensure individuals with significant security responsibilities understand their responsibilities in securing information systems; (6) assist agencies in identifying, assessing, prioritizing, and monitoring the progress of corrective efforts for security weaknesses found in programs and systems; (7) deter, detect, and defend against unauthorized network access; (8) ensure access rights are only given to the intended individuals

---

[15]The 11 information system control categories for inspectors general were: (1) risk management, (2) configuration management, (3) incident response and reporting, (4) security awareness training, (5) specialized training for security personnel, (6) remedial actions for identified weaknesses, (7) remote access to agency systems, (8) account and identity management, (9) continuous monitoring, (10) contingency planning, and (11) contractor systems.

or processes; (9) maintain a current security status for one or more information systems or for all information systems on which the organization's mission depends; (10) ensure agencies are adequately prepared to cope with the loss of operational capabilities due to a service disruption such as an act of nature, fire, accident, or sabotage; and (11) assist agencies in determining whether contractor-operated systems have adequate security.

Inspectors general reported that most agencies documented policies and procedures that were consistent with federal guidelines and requirements; however, several agencies had not fully documented policies and procedures for individual control categories. In addition, the number of agencies documenting policies and procedures increased for some control categories, but declined for others. For example, an increasing number of agencies documented policies and procedures for risk management, configuration management, and continuous monitoring, but the number of agencies documenting policies and procedures for security awareness and remote access declined. According to OMB, the decline in the number of agencies documenting certain policies and procedures could be due to agencies' not updating their policies and procedures after new federal requirements are established or new technologies are deployed. Table 1 provides a summary of the number of agencies that fully documented information security program policies and procedures for fiscal years 2011 and 2012.

Table 1: Number of the 24 Major Agencies that Fully Documented Information Security Program Policies and Procedures for Fiscal Years 2011 and 2012

Control category	2011	2012	Change
Risk Management			
Policies	17	20	+3
Procedures	15	20	+5
Configuration Management			
Policies	20	21	+1
Procedures	16	21	+5
Incident Response & Reporting			
Policies	23	19	-4
Procedures	20	19	-1
Security Awareness Training			
Policies	24	21	-3
Procedures	22	21	-1

GAO-13-776 Federal Information Security

Control category	2011	2012	Change
Specialized Training for Security Personnel			
Policies	22	21	-1
Procedures	19	21	+2
Remedial Actions for Identified Weaknesses			
Policies	21	20	-1
Procedures	17	20	+3
Remote Access to Agency Systems			
Policies	22	17	-5
Procedures	19	17	-2
Account & Identity Management			
Policies	21	19	-2
Procedures	15	19	+4
Continuous Monitoring			
Policies	16	20	+4
Procedures	12	20	+8
Contingency Planning			
Policies	21	20	-1
Procedures	18	16	-2
Contractor Systems			
Policies	21	20	-1
Procedures	19	20	+1

Source: GAO analysis of inspectors general FISMA reports for fiscal years 2011 and 2012.

Although most agencies documented security policies and procedures, they often did not fully or consistently implement them. To illustrate, most major federal agencies had weaknesses in the following information system controls:

- **Access controls:** In fiscal year 2012, almost all (23 of 24) of the major federal agencies had weaknesses in the controls that are intended to limit or detect access to computer resources (data, programs, equipment, and facilities), thereby protecting them against unauthorized modification, loss, and disclosure. For example, 21 of 24 agencies had weaknesses in their ability to appropriately identify and authenticate system users. To illustrate, although agencies are required to uniquely identify users on their systems, some users shared accounts at 1 agency, and administrators shared accounts for multiple systems at another agency, making it difficult for the agencies to account for user and administrator activity on their systems. Other agencies had weak password controls, including systems with passwords that had not been changed from the easily guessable default passwords supplied by the vendor. In addition, 20 of 24 agencies had weaknesses in the process used to grant or restrict user access to information technology resources. For example, 1 agency had not disabled 363 user accounts for individuals who were no longer employed by the agency, despite a department policy of disabling these accounts within 48 hours of an employee's departure. Further, 18 of 24 agencies had weaknesses in the protection of information system boundaries.[16] For example, although 1 agency had established a program for remote access to agency systems, it had not ensured that authentication mechanisms for remote access meet NIST guidelines for remote authentication. Lastly, 11 of 24 agencies had weaknesses in their ability to restrict physical access or harm to computer resources and protect them from unintentional loss or impairment. For example, 1 agency had not always deactivated physical access cards for contractors that no longer worked at the agency and had provided physical access to employees that were not approved for such access.

- **Configuration management:** In fiscal year 2012, all 24 agencies had weaknesses in the controls that are intended to prevent unauthorized changes to information system resources (for example, software programs and hardware configurations) and provide reasonable assurance that systems are configured and operating securely and as intended. For example, 20 of 24 agencies had weaknesses in processes for updating software to protect against known vulnerabilities. One agency had not installed critical updates in a timely manner for 14 of 15 systems residing on one if its networks reviewed by the agency's inspector general. Another agency had multiple database update-related vulnerabilities dating back to 2009. In addition, 17 of 24 agencies had weaknesses in authorizing, testing, approving, tracking, and controlling system changes. For example, most of the system change request records reviewed by 1 agency's independent auditor did not include the proper approvals for the system change.

- **Segregation of duties:** In fiscal year 2012, 18 of 24 agencies had weaknesses in the controls intended to prevent one individual from controlling all critical stages of a process, which is often achieved by

---

[16]Boundary protection is the monitoring and control of communications at the external boundary to prevent and detect malicious and other unauthorized communication.

splitting responsibilities between two or more organizational groups. For example, at 1 agency, excessive system access was granted to users of at least seven systems and may have allowed users to perform incompatible duties. The same agency also did not have an effective process for monitoring its systems for users with the ability to perform these incompatible duties.

Illustrating the extent to which weaknesses affect the 24 major federal agencies, inspectors general at 22 of 24 agencies cited information security as a major management challenge for their agency, and 19 agencies reported that information security control deficiencies were either a material weakness or significant deficiency[17] in internal controls over financial reporting in fiscal year 2012. Until all agencies properly document and implement policies and procedures, and implement recommendations made by us and inspectors general to correct weaknesses identified, they may not be able to effectively reduce risk to their information and information systems, and the information security practices that are driven by these policies and procedures may be applied inconsistently.

Agencies Generally Implemented Elements of Security Planning but Did Not Consistently Develop or Update Security Plans

FISMA requires an agency's information security program to include plans for providing adequate information security for networks, facilities, and systems or groups of information systems, as appropriate. According to NIST, the purpose of the system security plan is to provide an overview of the security requirements of the system and describe the controls in place or planned for meeting those requirements. The first step in the system security planning process is to categorize the system based on the impact to agency operations, assets, and personnel should the confidentiality, integrity, and availability of the agency information and information systems be compromised. This categorization is then used to determine the appropriate security controls needed for each system. Another key step is selecting a baseline of security controls for each system and documenting those controls in the security plan.

---

[17]A material weakness is a deficiency, or combination of deficiencies, that results in more than a remote likelihood that a material misstatement of the financial statements will not be prevented or detected. A significant deficiency is a deficiency, or combination of deficiencies, in internal control that is less severe that a material weakness, yet important enough to merit attention by those charged with governance. A control deficiency exists when the design or operation of a control does not allow management or employees, in the normal course of performing their assigned functions, to prevent or detect and correct misstatements on a timely basis.

In fiscal years 2011 and 2012, OMB asked inspectors general to report on whether their agency appropriately categorized information systems and selected appropriate baseline security controls. Although a few inspectors general reported weaknesses in their agency's process for categorizing information systems, 21 of 24 reported that agencies appropriately categorized them in fiscal years 2011 and 2012. In addition, in fiscal years 2011 and 2012, 18 of 24 inspectors general also stated that agencies selected an appropriately tailored set of baseline security controls.

However, inspectors general at 19 of 24 agencies reported that security plans were not always complete or properly updated. For example, 11 system security plans at 1 agency did not meet the minimum security requirements required by NIST 800-53.[18] Three components of another agency were not consistently updating system security plans to reflect the current operating environment. Further, 2 of the 16 system security plans reviewed at another agency had not been updated within the required 3-year period.

Until agencies appropriately develop and update system security plans and implement recommendations made by us and inspectors general to correct weaknesses identified, they may face an increased risk that officials will be unaware of system security requirements and that controls are not in place.

Agencies Declined in Providing Security Awareness Training but Improved in Providing Specialized Training

FISMA requires agencies to provide security awareness training to personnel, including contractors and other users of information systems that support the operations and assets of the agency. Training is intended to inform agency personnel of the information security risks associated with their activities, and their responsibilities in complying with agency policies and procedures designed to reduce these risks. FISMA also requires agencies to train and oversee personnel with significant security responsibilities for information security with respect to those responsibilities. Providing training to agency personnel is critical to securing information and information systems because people are one of the weakest links in attempts to secure systems and networks. In fiscal years 2011 and 2012, OMB required agencies to report on the number of

---

[18]NIST, *Recommended Security Controls for Federal Information Systems and Organizations,* NIST Special Publication 800-53 Revision 3 (Gaithersburg, Md.: August 2009). NIST updated this publication and released revision 4 in April 2013.

network users that were provided and successfully completed security awareness training for that year. Agencies were also required to report on the number of network users and other staff with significant security responsibilities that were provided specialized training.

In fiscal year 2012, 12 of the 24 agencies provided annual security awareness training to at least 90 percent of their network users, which is a notable decline from fiscal year 2011, in which 22 of 24 agencies provided training to at least 90 percent of their users. Inspectors general at 17 of 24 agencies also reported weaknesses in security awareness programs, including agencies' ability to track the number of system users provided training that year. For example, 5 of 24 inspectors general reported that their agency's process for identifying and tracking the status of security awareness training was not adequate or in accordance with government policies, an improvement over 10 of 24 in fiscal year 2011. To illustrate, in fiscal year 2011, 1 agency could not identify evidence of security awareness training for over 12 percent of system users at three component agencies. Another agency lacked a process to ensure all contractors were identified and provided with security awareness training in fiscal year 2012. Without sufficiently trained security personnel, security lapses are more likely to occur and could contribute to further information security weaknesses.

In fiscal year 2012, 16 of 24 agencies provided specialized training to at least 90 percent of their users with significant security responsibilities, a slight increase from 15 of 24 in fiscal year 2011. In addition, inspectors general reported in fiscal year 2012 that 22 of 24 agencies established a specialized training program that complied with FISMA, an improvement over fiscal year 2011, in which half of the major federal agencies had established such a program. Further, in fiscal year 2012, 19 of 24 inspectors general reported that their agency's mechanism for tracking individuals who need specialized training was adequate, a slight improvement from fiscal year 2011, in which 17 of 24 reported adequate tracking.

Although the number of agencies implementing specialized training programs increased, 16 of 24 inspectors general identified weaknesses with such programs in fiscal year 2012. For example, 1 agency had not yet defined "significant information security responsibilities" in order to identify those individuals requiring specialized training. Another agency's specialized training process was ad hoc and everyone with significant security responsibilities had taken the same training course, not one that was tailored for their specific job roles. While agencies have made progress in implementing specialized training programs that comply with

FISMA, without tailoring training to specific job roles agencies are at increased risk that individuals with significant security responsibilities may not be adequately prepared to perform their specific responsibilities in protecting the agency's information and information systems.

Most Agencies Established a Test and Evaluation Program and Are Working toward Establishing Continuous Monitoring Programs

FISMA requires that federal agencies periodically test and evaluate the effectiveness of their information security policies, procedures, and practices as part of implementing an agency-wide security program. This testing is to be performed with a frequency depending on risk, but no less than annually. Testing should include management, operational, and technical controls for every system identified in the agency's required inventory of major systems. This type of oversight is a fundamental element that demonstrates management's commitment to the security program, reminds employees of their roles and responsibilities, and identifies and mitigates areas of noncompliance and ineffectiveness. Although control tests and evaluations may encourage compliance with security policies, the full benefits are not achieved unless the results are used to improve security. In recent years, the federal government has been moving toward implementing a more frequent control testing process called continuous monitoring. In March 2012, the White House Cybersecurity Coordinator announced that his office, in coordination with experts from DHS, the Department of Defense (DOD), and OMB, had identified continuous monitoring of federal information systems as a cross-agency priority area for improving federal cybersecurity. According to NIST, the goal of continuous monitoring is to transform the otherwise static test and evaluation process into a dynamic risk mitigation program that provides essential, near real-time security status and remediation. In February 2010, NIST included continuous monitoring as one of six steps in its risk management framework described in NIST special publication 800-37.[19] In addition, in September 2011 NIST published special publication 800-137 to assist organizations in the development of a continuous monitoring strategy and the implementation of a continuous monitoring program that provides awareness of threats and

---

[19]NIST, *Guide for Applying the Risk Management Framework to Federal Information Systems,* NIST Special Publication 800-37 Revision 1 (Gaithersburg, Md.: February 2010).

vulnerabilities, visibility into organizational assets, and the effectiveness of implemented security controls.[20]

Test and Evaluation Programs Were Generally Established

The majority of federal agencies implemented elements of test and evaluation programs in fiscal years 2011 and 2012. For fiscal year 2012, 17 of 24 inspectors general reported that agencies assessed controls using appropriate assessment procedures to determine the extent to which controls are implemented correctly, operating as intended, and producing the desired outcome with respect to meeting the security requirements for the system.

However, 17 of 24 inspectors general also identified weaknesses in agencies' processes for testing and evaluating identified controls. For example, 10 of 23[21] agencies did not monitor information security controls on an ongoing basis in fiscal year 2012. According to DHS, monitoring information security controls includes assessing control effectiveness, documenting changes to the system or its environment of operation, conducting security impact analyses of the associated changes, and reporting the security state of the system to designated organizational officials. One agency had not performed ongoing assessments of selected security controls on nearly 10 percent of its systems in fiscal year 2012. Another agency had not met the basic test and evaluation requirement for the past 5 years, and this was the major reason the agency's inspector general classified its information security governance as a material weakness for financial reporting. The identified weaknesses in test and evaluation programs could limit agencies' awareness of vulnerabilities in their critical information systems.

Progress Made in Implementing Continuous Monitoring Programs

According to OMB's annual report to Congress, agencies reported improvements in fiscal year 2012 in implementing tools that provided automated continuous monitoring capabilities for vulnerability, configuration, and asset management for the agency's information

---

[20]NIST, *Information Security Continuous Monitoring (ISCM) for Federal Information Systems and Organizations,* NIST Special Publication 800-137 (Gaithersburg, Md.: September 2011).

[21]The Department of Commerce Office of Inspector General did not access this metric in fiscal year 2012.

systems.[22] The annual DHS reporting metrics established a minimum goal of 80 percent for implementing an automated capability to assess vulnerability, configuration, and asset management information for agencies' information technology assets in fiscal year 2012. According to OMB, 17 of 24 major federal agencies reported at least 80 percent implementation of this capability for asset and configuration management, and 16 of 24 reported at least 80 percent implementation of this capability for vulnerability management. In addition, as figure 2 illustrates, most agencies reported an overall improvement in the percentage of information technology assets with these automated capabilities from fiscal year 2011 to 2012. Specifically, 12 agencies increased the percentage of information technology assets with automated capabilities for asset management, 18 agencies increased the percentage of information technology assets with automated capabilities for configuration management, and 14 agencies increased the percentage of information technology assets with automated capabilities for vulnerability management.

---

[22]Automated vulnerability management capabilities could include active vulnerability scanners, reports from software that can self-report information that can be used to identify vulnerabilities, or a combination of several methods for identifying vulnerabilities. Automated configuration management capabilities provide the ability to compare the current system's configuration to a baseline configuration using, among other things, configuration scanners or reports from software. Automated asset management capabilities use computer systems to provide information on the agency's asset inventory.

Figure 2: Agency Implementation of Automated Asset, Configuration, and Vulnerability Monitoring Capabilities from Fiscal Year 2011 to Fiscal Year 2012

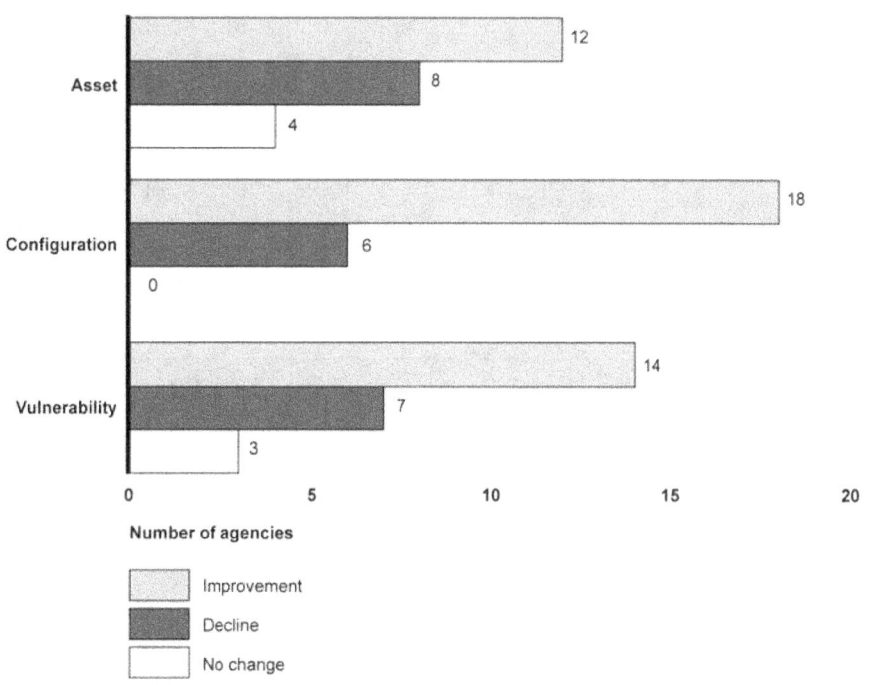

Source: GAO analysis of inspectors general FISMA reports for fiscal years 2011 and 2012

Although many agencies improved in implementing these continuous monitoring capabilities, several agencies declined. For example, in fiscal year 2011, DOD reported 95 percent implementation of configuration management capabilities. However, in fiscal year 2012 its capabilities declined to 53 percent. According to OMB, DOD's decline was due to a change in the reporting criteria for the configuration management metrics. In addition, the Department of Agriculture reported 100 percent capability for asset management continuous monitoring in fiscal year 2011, but that capability dropped to 69 percent in fiscal year 2012. OMB officials stated that they did not know the reason for the decline.

Inspectors general also reported improvements made by agencies. For example, 17 of 24 agencies established an enterprise-wide continuous monitoring program that assessed the security state of information systems, an improvement over fiscal year 2011, in which 9 agencies had established such a program. In addition, in fiscal year 2012, 16 of 24 agencies documented a strategy and plans for continuous monitoring, an improvement from 11 in fiscal year 2011.

Although these were improvements over fiscal year 2011, many agencies had continuous monitoring programs that did not comply with NIST and OMB guidance. For example, in fiscal year 2012, 10 agencies were not conducting assessments of security controls based on continuous monitoring plans. Of the 10 agencies that did not conduct assessments of security controls based on a continuous monitoring plan, most agencies did not have a documented strategy or plan for continuous monitoring in fiscal year 2012. Until agencies fully implement continuous monitoring programs, the full benefit of having ongoing insight into security control effectiveness will be difficult to achieve.

Agencies Declined in Implementing Elements of Remediation Programs

FISMA requires agencies to plan, implement, evaluate, and document remedial actions to address any deficiencies in their information security policies, procedures, and practices. In its fiscal year 2012 FISMA reporting instructions, OMB emphasized that remedial action plans—known as plans of action and milestones (POA&M)—are to be the authoritative agency-wide management tool, inclusive of all evaluations. In addition, NIST guidance states that federal agencies should develop a POA&M for information systems to document the organization's planned remedial actions to correct weaknesses or deficiencies noted during the assessment of the security controls and to reduce or eliminate known vulnerabilities in the system. NIST guidance also states that organizations should update existing POA&Ms based on the findings from security controls assessments, security impact analyses, and continuous monitoring activities. According to OMB, remediation plans assist agencies in identifying, assessing, prioritizing, and monitoring the progress of corrective efforts for security weaknesses found in programs and systems. In fiscal years 2011 and 2012, inspectors general were required to report on agency remediation programs, including policies and procedures; the agency's ability to track, prioritize, and remediate weaknesses; whether the agency establishes and adheres to milestone remediation dates; and whether the remediation plans are effective for correcting weaknesses.

Most major federal agencies implemented remediation programs in fiscal years 2011 and 2012. Specifically, in fiscal year 2012, inspectors general reported that 19 of 24 agencies established remediation programs consistent with FISMA requirements. Additionally, in fiscal year 2012, 20 of 24 agencies had documented procedures for managing IT security weaknesses discovered during security control assessments, an increase over 17 of 24 in fiscal year 2011.

Although most agencies had established a remediation program that included documented procedures, several agencies declined in implementing elements of their program. For example, 15 of 24 inspectors general reported that their agencies were appropriately tracking, prioritizing, and remediating identified weaknesses, a decline from the 20 of 24 that were appropriately tracking identified weaknesses, 21 of 24 that were appropriately prioritizing weaknesses, and 17 of 24 that were appropriately remediating identified weaknesses in fiscal year 2011. In addition, in fiscal year 2012, 12 of 24 agencies established and adhered to milestone remediation dates, which is also a decline from 14 of 24 in fiscal year 2011. One agency's remediation plan showed that 58 percent of the documented control weaknesses were overdue for remediation by more than 90 days, and 235 weaknesses were over 2-years old. Figure 3 illustrates agencies' general decline in implementing several elements of comprehensive remediation programs from fiscal year 2011 to 2012. Without a sound remediation process, agencies cannot be assured that information security weaknesses are being corrected and managed.

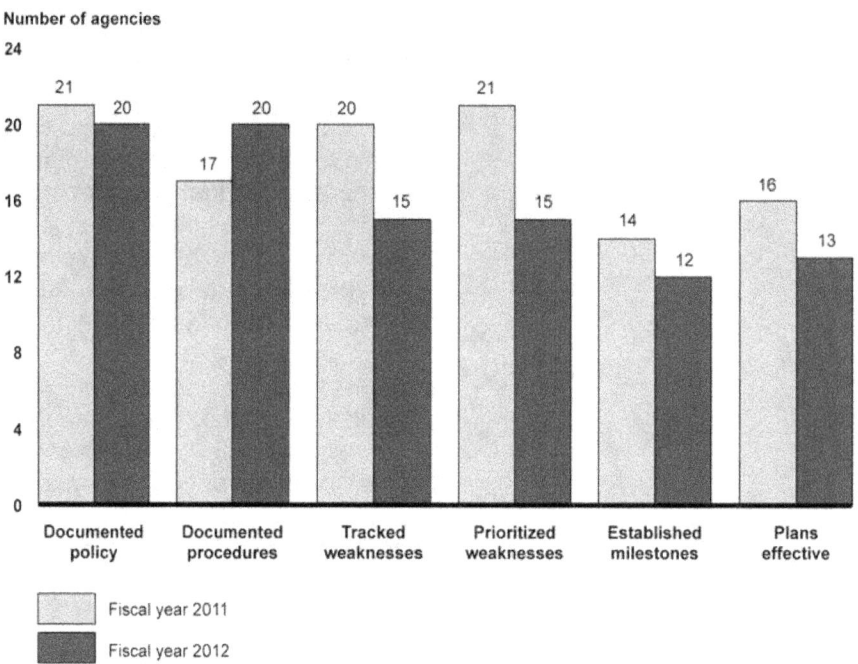

Figure 3: Agency Implementation of Remediation Program Elements in Fiscal Years 2011 and 2012

Number of agencies

Element	Fiscal year 2011	Fiscal year 2012
Documented policy	21	20
Documented procedures	17	20
Tracked weaknesses	20	15
Prioritized weaknesses	21	15
Established milestones	14	12
Plans effective	16	13

Source: GAO analysis of inspectors general FISMA reports for fiscal years 2011 and 2012.

Most Agencies Developed an Incident Response and Reporting Program

FISMA requires that agency security programs include procedures for detecting, reporting, and responding to security incidents and that agencies report incidents to US-CERT. According to NIST, incident response capabilities are necessary for rapidly detecting incidents, minimizing loss and destruction, mitigating the weaknesses that were exploited, and restoring computing services.[23] US-CERT has established specific time frames for reporting incidents.

In fiscal year 2012, 20 of 23 inspectors general reported that their agency had implemented an incident response and reporting program that is

---

[23]NIST, *Computer Security Incident Handling Guide*, Special Publication 800-61 Revision 2 (Gaithersburg, Md.: August 2012).

consistent with FISMA, OMB policy, and applicable NIST guidelines.[24] This is an increase over fiscal year 2011 reporting in which 16 of 24 agencies had programs that did not require significant improvements. Although more agencies implemented such a program, fewer agencies documented policies and procedures for incident detection, reporting, and response—the foundation of the program. Specifically, 19 of 23 agencies had documented policies and procedures in fiscal year 2012, while in fiscal year 2011, 23 of 24 agencies documented policies, and 20 of 24 documented procedures. In addition, 19 of 23 agencies performed a comprehensive analysis, validation, and documentation of incidents in fiscal year 2012, an improvement of 3 agencies over fiscal year 2011. Table 2 shows agency progress in implementing incident detection, reporting, and response programs and related activities in fiscal years 2011 and 2012.

Table 2: Agency Progress in Implementing Incident Detection, Reporting, and Response Program and Related Activities from Fiscal Year 2011 to Fiscal Year 2012

Program/Activity	Number of agencies		
	Fiscal year 2011	Fiscal year 2012	Improvement/Decline
Established a program for detecting, responding to, and reporting incidents consistent with requirements	16 of 24	20 of 23[a]	Improvement
Documentation of policies for detecting, responding to, and reporting incidents	23 of 24	19 of 23[a]	Decline
Documentation of procedures for detecting, responding to, and reporting incidents	20 of 24	19 of 23[a]	Decline
Comprehensive analysis, validation, and documentation of incidents	16 of 24	19 of 23[a]	Improvement

Source: GAO analysis of agency documentation and responses by agency inspectors general to fiscal year 2011 and 2012.

[a]One agency did not evaluate this information security program element in fiscal year 2012.

Most major federal agencies are reporting and resolving security incidents within established time frames; however, the number of agencies that routinely reported security incidents to US-CERT within established time frames declined from fiscal year 2011 to fiscal year 2012. Specifically, in fiscal year 2012 inspectors general reported that 18 of 23 agencies reported incidents, when applicable, to US-CERT within established time frames, a slight decline from fiscal year 2011 in which 19 of 24 agencies

---

[24]The Department of Commerce Office of Inspector General did not assess incident detection, reporting, and response reporting metrics for fiscal year 2012.

GAO-13-776 Federal Information Security

reported in a timely manner. In addition, 31 of 75 incidents selected for review were not reported to US-CERT within the required time frame, 18 of which were the result of a lost or stolen device. Agencies remained consistent in their efforts to report incidents to law enforcement. Specifically, in fiscal years 2011 and 2012, 20 agencies appropriately reported such incidents.

Agencies also made improvements in responding to and resolving incidents. Specifically, inspectors general reported in fiscal year 2012 that 18 of 23 agencies responded to and resolved incidents in a timely manner, an improvement from fiscal year 2011, in which 15 of 24 agencies did so. Table 3 summarizes agency incident reporting and response practices for fiscal year 2011 and 2012.

Table 3: Agency Incident Reporting and Response Practices in Fiscal Years 2011 and 2012

Practice	Number of agencies		
	Fiscal year 2011	Fiscal year 2012	Improvement/Decline
The agency reports to US-CERT within established time frames.	19 of 24	18 of 23[a]	Decline
The agency reports to law enforcement within established time frames.	20 of 24	20 of 23 [a]	No change
The agency responds to and resolves incidents in a timely manner, as specified in organization policy or standards, to minimize further damage.	19 of 24	18 of 23 [a]	Undetermined [a]

Source: GAO analysis of responses by agency inspectors general to fiscal year 2011 and 2012 FISMA reporting questions.

[a]One agency did not evaluate this information security program element in fiscal year 2012.

In addition to responding to incidents, agencies also took action to remediate vulnerabilities or implement recommendations in response to vulnerability alerts.[25] Specifically, in fiscal years 2011 and 2012, 22 agencies reported that they had remediated vulnerabilities or implemented recommendations for over 90 percent of the vulnerability alerts they received during that time period.

---

[25]US-CERT provides agencies with security awareness reports that communicate broad assessments of threats and inform agencies of actionable recommendations for monitoring and responding to suspicious activity. The Department of Defense also issues similar alerts called information assurance vulnerability alerts.

Rising Number of Incidents Reported by Federal Agencies Highlights the Need for Strong Incident Detection, Reporting, and Response Programs

Federal agencies have reported increasing numbers of cybersecurity incidents that have placed sensitive information at risk, with potentially serious impacts on federal operations, assets, and people. The increasing risks to federal systems underscore the importance of a robust incident detection, reporting, and response program and are demonstrated by the dramatic increase in reports of security incidents, the ease of obtaining and using hacking tools, and steady advances in the sophistication and effectiveness of attack technology. As shown in figure 4, over the past 6 years the number of incidents reported by federal agencies to US-CERT has increased from 5,503 in fiscal year 2006 to 48,562 incidents in fiscal year 2012, an increase of 782 percent.

Figure 4: Incidents Reported to US-CERT by Federal Agencies in Fiscal Years 2006-2012

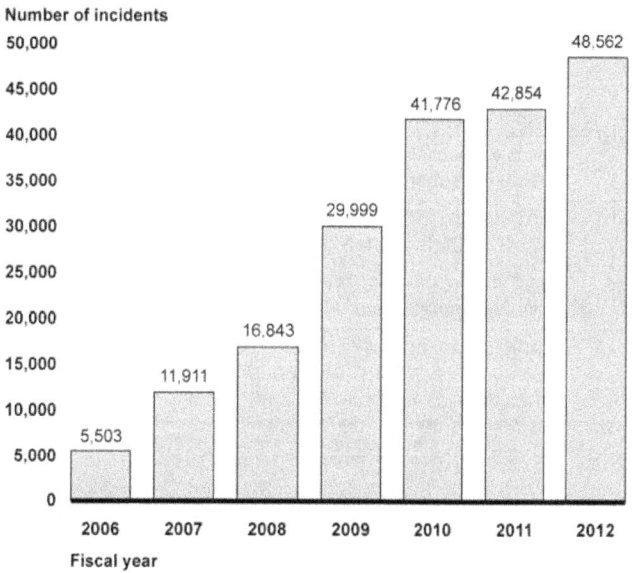

Source: GAO analysis of US-CERT data for fiscal years 2006-2012.

Of the incidents reported in 2012, 46,043 were reported by the 24 major federal agencies. Table 4 describes the incident categories as defined by US-CERT.

Table 4: US-CERT Fiscal Year 2012 Incident Categories and Definitions

Category/Subcategory	Definition
Unauthorized Access	Unauthorized access is used to categorize all incidents where an unprivileged user gains or may have gained control of a system or resource. Equipment is a specific subset of this category.
Equipment	This subset of unauthorized access is used for all incidents involving lost, stolen, or confiscated equipment, including mobile devices, laptops, backup disks, or removable media.
Denial of Service	This category is used for all successful denial of service attacks, such as a flood of traffic that renders a web server unavailable to legitimate users.
Malicious Code	Used for all successful executions or installations of malicious software that are not immediately quarantined and cleaned by preventative measures such as anti-virus tools.
Improper Usage	Improper usage is used to categorize all incidents where a user violates acceptable computing policies or rules of behavior. These include spillage of information from one classification level to another. Policy violation is a specific subset of this category.
Policy Violation	This subset of improper usage is primarily used to categorize incidents of mishandling data in storage or transit, such as digital personally identifiable information (PII) records or procurement-sensitive information found unsecured or PII being e-mailed without proper encryption.
Social Engineering	Social engineering is used to categorize fraudulent websites and other attempts to entice users to provide sensitive information or download malicious code. Phishing is a subset of social engineering.
Phishing	This is a specific subset of social engineering which is used to categorize phishing incidents and campaigns reported directly to phishing-report@us-cert.gov from both the public and private sectors.
Suspicious Network Activity	This category is primarily used for incident reports and notifications created from EINSTEIN and EINSTEIN 2[a] data analyzed by US-CERT.
Non Cyber	Non Cyber is used for filing all reports of PII spillages or possible mishandling of PII that involve hard copies or printed material rather than digital records.
Other	For the purposes of this report, a separate superset of multiple subcategories has been employed to accommodate several low-frequency types of incident reports, such as unconfirmed third-party notifications, failed brute force attempts, port scans, or reported incidents where the cause is unknown.

Source: Office of Management and Budget's Fiscal Year 2012 Report to Congress on the Implementation of the Federal Information Security Management Act of 2002.

[a]EINSTEIN 1 analyzes network flow information from participating federal executive government agencies and provides a high-level perspective from which to observe potential malicious activity in computer network traffic of participating agencies' computer networks. The updated version, EINSTEIN 2, incorporates network intrusion detection technology capable of alerting US-CERT to the presence of malicious or potentially harmful computer network activity in federal executive agencies' network traffic.

As indicated in figure 5, the three most prevalent types of incidents reported to US-CERT during fiscal year 2012 were those involving spillage or mishandling of personally identifiable information involving hard copies or printed material rather than digital records (non cyber), policy violations, and execution or installation of malicious software. Incidents involving personally identifiable information at the 24 major federal agencies increased 110 percent, from 10,207 in fiscal year 2009 to 21,459 in fiscal year 2012.

Figure 5: Incidents Reported by the 24 Major Federal Agencies in Fiscal Year 2012 by Category

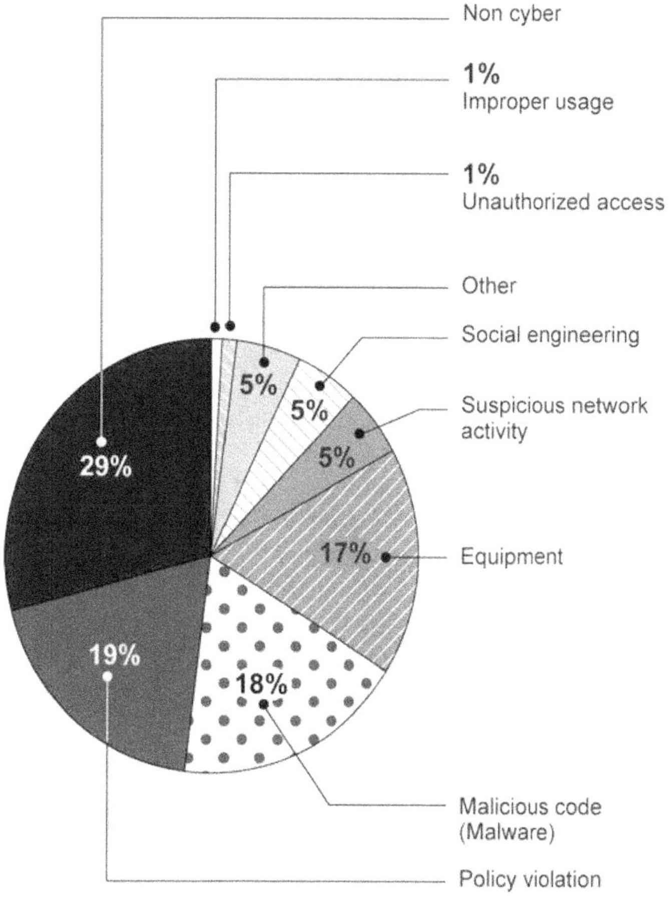

- Non cyber
- 1% Improper usage
- 1% Unauthorized access
- Other
- Social engineering
- 5%
- 5%
- Suspicious network activity
- 5%
- 29%
- 17% Equipment
- 19%
- 18%
- Malicious code (Malware)
- Policy violation

Source: GAO analysis of Fiscal Year 2012 Report to Congress on the Implementation of The Federal Information Security Management Act of 2002

Reported attacks and unintentional incidents involving federal systems demonstrate that a serious attack could be devastating. Agencies have experienced a wide range of incidents involving data loss or theft, computer intrusions, and privacy breaches, underscoring the importance of strong security practices. The following examples reported in 2011 and 2012 illustrate that a broad array of information and assets remain at risk.

- In May 2012, the Federal Retirement Thrift Investment Board[26] reported a sophisticated cyber attack on the computer of a third party that provided services to the Thrift Savings Plan (TSP).[27] As a result of the attack, approximately 123,000 TSP participants had their personal information accessed. According to the board, the information included 43,587 individuals' names, addresses, and Social Security numbers; and 79,614 individuals' Social Security numbers and other TSP-related information.

- The National Aeronautics and Space Administration (NASA) inspector general testified in February 2012 that computers with Chinese-based Internet protocol addresses had gained full access to key systems at the agency's Jet Propulsion Laboratory, enabling attackers to modify, copy, or delete sensitive files; create user accounts for mission-critical laboratory systems; and upload hacking tools to steal user credentials and compromise other NASA systems.[28] These individuals were also able to modify system logs to conceal their actions.

- In March 2011, attackers breached the networks of RSA, the Security Division of EMC Corporation,[29] and, according to the company, obtained information about network authentication tokens for a U.S. military contractor. In May 2011, attackers used this information to breach the contractor's security systems containing sensitive weapons information and military technology. EMC published information about the breach and the immediate steps customers could take to strengthen the security of their systems.

These incidents illustrate the serious impact that cyber attacks can have on federal and military operations, critical infrastructure, and the

---

[26]The Federal Retirement Thrift Investment Board is an independent agency in the executive branch governed by five presidentially appointed board members and is respons ble for administering the Thrift Savings Plan (TSP).

[27]TSP is a tax-deferred defined contribution savings plan for federal employees similar to the 401(k) plans offered by private employers.

[28]Paul K. Martin, Inspector General, National Aeronautics and Space Administration, "NASA Cybersecurity: An Examination of the Agency's Information Security," testimony before the Subcommittee on Investigations and Oversight, Committee on Science, Space, and Technology, House of Representatives (Washington, D.C.: Feb. 29, 2012).

[29]The RSA SecureID system is a two-factor authentication solution providing secure access to remote and mobile users.

confidentiality, integrity, and availability of sensitive government, private sector, and personal information. Effectively implementing a comprehensive incident detection, reporting, and response program would help agencies better protect their information and information systems from attack.

Agencies Declined in Implementing Elements of Continuity of Operations Programs

FISMA requires federal agencies to implement plans and procedures to ensure continuity of operations for information systems that support the operations and assets of the agency. According to NIST, contingency planning is part of overall information system continuity of operations planning, which fits into a much broader security and emergency management effort that includes, among other things, organizational and business process continuity and disaster recovery planning. These plans and procedures are essential steps in ensuring that agencies are adequately prepared to cope with the loss of operational capabilities due to a service disruption such as an act of nature, fire, accident, or sabotage. According to NIST, these plans should cover all key functions, including assessing an agency's information technology and identifying resources, minimizing potential damage and interruption, developing and documenting the plan, and testing it and making necessary adjustments.

According to inspectors general, 18 of the 23 major federal agencies had established a business continuity and disaster recovery program that was consistent with FISMA requirements, OMB policy, and applicable NIST guidelines in fiscal year 2012.[30] However, although most agencies established a program, the number of agencies that fully implemented certain key elements of such a program declined. For example, in both fiscal years 2011 and 2012, about half of the agencies did not conduct a business impact analysis for their information systems. A business impact analysis facilitates the prioritization of systems and their processes based on categorization levels in order to develop priority recovery strategies to minimize loss. Specifically, in fiscal year 2012, 12 of 23 agencies had not performed an overall business impact analysis, a slight decline from 11 of 24 in fiscal year 2011. In addition, in fiscal year 2012, 8 of 23 agencies had not documented business continuity and disaster recovery plans. Even with the existence of plans, 21 inspectors general reported weaknesses in agencies' comprehensive contingency planning processes

---

[30]The Department of Commerce Office of Inspector General did not assess continuity of operations metrics for fiscal year 2012.

in fiscal year 2012. For example, 9 of 1 agency's 13 components had at least one information system that did not have a business continuity and disaster recovery plan. Another agency's controls were not adequate to ensure that the organization developed and implemented a contingency plan addressing activities associated with restoring an information system after a disruption or failure. Table 5 provides a summary of inspectors general assessments of continuity of operations programs for fiscal years 2011 and 2012.

Table 5: Number of the 24 Major Agencies Implementing Key Elements of Continuity of Operations Programs for Fiscal Years 2011 and 2012

Key continuity of operations program element	Fiscal year 2011		Fiscal year 2012		
	Implemented	Not implemented	Implemented	Not implemented	Improvement/Decline
Business impact analysis	13	11	11	12[a]	Decline
Development of business continuity/disaster recovery plan	19	5	15	8[a]	Decline
Development of test, training and exercise programs	19	5	16	7[a]	Decline
Testing of system-specific contingency plans	16	8	15	8[a]	No change

Source: GAO analysis of inspectors general FISMA reports for fiscal years 2011 and 2012.

[a]One agency did not evaluate this information security program element in fiscal year 2012.

Further, several agencies lacked other important elements of a continuity of operations program. For example, 9 of 23 agencies were not regularly testing disaster recovery and business continuity plans, and the reports developed after plan testing did not include issues discovered during the test. One agency had not tested contingency plans for 53 percent of the systems documented in its system inventory in a timely manner. Another agency did not summarize results or lessons learned in several after-action reports. Further, 9 of 23 agencies did not have alternate processing sites for some systems. Lastly, although NIST recommended that contingency plans include the supply chain, 8 of 23 agencies had not included threats to the supply chain in the contingency planning process.

The uneven implementation of a comprehensive continuity of operations program and weaknesses identified by inspectors general could lead to less effective recovery efforts and may prevent a successful and timely system recovery when service disruptions occur.

GAO-13-776 Federal Information Security

OMB and DHS Continue to Take Actions Aimed at Improving Federal Information Security, but Additional Steps Are Needed

FISMA requires OMB to develop and oversee the implementation of policies, standards, and guidelines on information security at executive branch agencies and to annually report to Congress on agency compliance with FISMA no later than March 1 of each year. In 2010, OMB assigned certain responsibilities to DHS including overseeing and assisting government efforts to provide adequate, risk-based, and cost-effective cybersecurity. Since our last report,[31] OMB and DHS have taken a number of actions intended to improve oversight of FISMA implementation and federal information security. These include the following activities, among others:

- **Cross-agency cybersecurity priority goals:** In 2012, the Cybersecurity Coordinator led an effort intended to focus federal agencies' cybersecurity activity on the most effective controls. His office, in coordination with federal cybersecurity experts from DHS, DOD, and OMB, identified three priority areas for strengthening federal cybersecurity, which were included in the DHS reporting metrics for fiscal year 2012:

  - *Trusted Internet connections*: Consolidate external telecommunication connections and ensure a set of baseline security capabilities for situational awareness and enhanced monitoring.

  - *Continuous monitoring of federal information systems*: Transform the otherwise static security control assessment and authorization process into a dynamic risk mitigation program that provides essential, near real-time security status and remediation, increasing visibility into system operations and helping security personnel make risk management decisions based on increased situational awareness.

  - *Strong authentication*: Increase the use of federal smartcard credentials such as Personal Identity Verification and Common Access Cards that provide multifactor authentication and digital signature and encryption capabilities, authorizing users to access federal information systems with a higher level of assurance.

---

[31]GAO-12-137.

- **CyberStat reviews:** In fiscal year 2011, DHS, along with OMB and National Security Staff (NSS),[32] conducted the first CyberStat reviews of seven federal agencies. According to OMB, these CyberStat reviews were face-to-face, evidence-based meetings to ensure agencies were accountable for their cybersecurity posture and assist them in developing focused strategies for improving their information security posture in areas where they were facing challenges. According to OMB, these reviews resulted in a prioritized action plan for the agency to improve overall agency performance. CyberStat reviews were also conducted for seven agencies in fiscal year 2012. According to OMB, these meetings focused heavily on the three administration priorities and not specifically on FISMA requirements. The top challenges raised by agencies in fiscal year 2012 included the need to upgrade legacy systems to support new capabilities, acquire skilled staff, and ensure that the necessary financial resources were allocated to the administration's priority initiatives for cybersecurity. According to DHS, OMB and NSS are now requiring a CyberStat review of all 24 major federal agencies for fiscal year 2013—a new process that began in December 2012. However, in May 2013 OMB officials stated that while conducting CyberStat reviews of all 24 agencies is their goal, they would not meet that goal this year, and in July 2013 DHS officials stated that they do not have the capacity to meet with all 24 agencies in 1 fiscal year.

- **CIO and CISO interviews:** In fiscal year 2011, DHS began interviewing agency CIO's and chief information security officers (CISO) on their agency's cybersecurity posture. According to OMB, these interviews had three distinct goals: (1) assessing the agency's FISMA compliance and challenges, (2) identifying security best practices and raising awareness of FISMA reporting requirements, and (3) establishing meaningful dialogue with the agency's senior leadership.

- **Baseline metrics:** Many of the fiscal year 2010 metrics were carried over into fiscal year 2011, which established a baseline and provided an opportunity to measure progress in federal agencies and the federal government as a whole. According to OMB, establishing these baseline metrics has improved their understanding of the current

---

[32]The National Security Staff are the professional staff who support the President's National Security Advisor and the National Security Council.

cybersecurity posture and helped to drive accountability for improving the collective effectiveness of the federal government's cybersecurity capabilities.

DHS Continues to Develop Reporting Metrics, but Additional Revisions Could Be Made

In our 2009 report on efforts needed to improve federal performance measures,[33] we found that leading organizations and experts have identified different types of measures that are useful in helping to achieve information security goals:

- **Compliance measures**, which are used to determine the extent to which security controls were in place that adhered to internal policies, industry standards, or other legal or regulatory requirements. These measures are effective at pointing out where improvements are needed in implementing required policies and procedures but provide only limited insight into the overall performance of an organization's information security program.

- **Control effectiveness measures**, which characterize the extent to which specific control activities within an organization's information security program meet their objectives. Rather than merely capturing what controls are in place, such measures gauge how effectively the controls have been implemented.

These categories are consistent with those laid out by NIST in its information security performance measurement guide,[34] which serves as official guidance on information security measures for federal agencies and which OMB requires agencies to follow. In addition, information security experts, as well as NIST guidance, indicated that organizations with increasingly effective information security programs should migrate from predominantly using compliance measures toward a balanced set of measures to include various types of measures.

Further, we found that measures generally have key characteristics and attributes.[35] For example, measures are most meaningful to an organization when they, among other things, had targets or thresholds for

---

[33]GAO, *Information Security: Concerted Effort Needed to Improve Federal Performance Measures,* GAO-09-617 (Washington, D.C.: Sept. 14, 2009).

[34]NIST, Special Publication 800-55 Revision 1, *Performance Measurement Guide for Information Security* (Gaithersburg, Md.: July 2008).

[35]GAO-09-617.

each measure to track progress over time and are linked to organizational priorities.

In our report we recommended that OMB, among other things, revise annual reporting guidance to agencies to require (1) reporting on a balanced set of measures, including measures that focus on the effectiveness of control activities and program impact; and (2) inclusion of all key attributes in the development of measures. OMB concurred with our recommendations and revised its fiscal year 2010 reporting instructions and metrics accordingly.

For fiscal years 2011 and 2012, DHS, as part of its recently assigned responsibilities for FISMA oversight, developed a revised set of reporting metrics to assess agencies' compliance with the act. Specifically, inspectors general were asked to report on 11 information system control categories, and agency chief information officers were asked to report on 12 categories, as indicated in table 6.

Table 6: Information System Control Categories Reported by Inspectors General and Agency Chief Information Officers

Information system control category	Inspectors general	CIOs
Risk management	X	
Configuration management	X	X
Incident response and reporting	X	X
Security training	X	X
Remediation programs (POA&M)	X	
Remote access management	X	X
Identity and access management	X	X
Continuous monitoring management	X	X
Contingency planning	X	
Contractor systems	X	
Security capital planning	X	
System inventory		X
Asset management		X
Vulnerability management		X
Data protection		X
Boundary protection		X
Network security protocols		X

Source: GAO analysis of DHS reporting metrics.

For each category, inspectors general and chief information officers were required to answer a series of questions related to the agency's implementation of these controls.

DHS Has Established Compliance Metrics for Most, but Not All FISMA Requirements for Agency Security Programs

The metrics developed for inspectors general and chief information officers by DHS for fiscal year 2012 address compliance with six of the eight components of an information security program as required by FISMA. Specifically, the metrics address the establishment of information security policies and procedures; security training; periodic testing and evaluation of the effectiveness of information security policies, procedures, and practices; remedial actions to address information security deficiencies; procedures for detecting, reporting, and responding to security incidents; and continuity of operations plans and procedures. However, these metrics do not specifically discuss two of the eight components—agencies' processes for conducting risk assessments or developing security plans. For example, while the metrics ask inspectors general to report on their agency's policies and procedures for risk management and its overall risk management program, they do not specifically require inspectors general or agency chief information officers to report on whether the agency has periodically assessed the risk and magnitude of harm that could result from the compromise of information and information systems that support the operations and assets of the agency, as required by FISMA. The metrics also do not specifically require agencies or inspectors general to comment on the development, documentation, and implementation of subordinate plans for providing adequate security for networks, facilities, and systems or groups of systems, as appropriate. Without measuring agencies' compliance with these FISMA requirements, DHS, OMB, and other stakeholders will have less insight into the implementation of agencies' information security programs.

Inspector General Reporting Did Not Consistently Capture the Effectiveness of Agency Programs

As highlighted in our 2009 report,[36] the use of control effectiveness measures in addition to compliance measures can provide additional insight into how effectively control activities are meeting their security objectives. According to OMB instructions for FISMA reporting, the DHS metrics for inspectors general were also designed to measure the effectiveness of agencies' information security programs, and OMB relied on responses by inspectors general to these metrics to gauge the effectiveness of information security programs.

While some of the metrics for inspectors general were intended to measure effectiveness, many of them did not. The 2012 metrics ask inspectors general to determine whether or not their agency has established a program for each of the 11 information system control categories, and whether or not these programs include key security practices. Several of these metrics were intended to reflect the effectiveness of agencies' program practices within the control categories. For example, for the incident response and reporting category, inspectors general were asked whether their agency responded to and resolved incidents in a timely manner and whether it reported incidents to US-CERT and law enforcement within established time frames. However, many of the metrics for inspectors general did not provide a means of assessing the effectiveness of the program for control categories. Specifically, the metrics focus on the establishment of the program but do not require inspectors general to characterize the extent to which these program components meet their objectives. For each control category, the metrics ask whether the agency established an enterprise-wide program that was consistent with FISMA requirements, OMB policy, and applicable NIST guidelines. However, these metrics do not allow the inspectors general to respond on how effectively the program is operating. Instead, they capture whether programs have been established.

The lack of effectiveness metrics has led to inconsistencies in inspector general reporting. The following examples illustrate that while inspectors general reported, via responses to the DHS metrics, that their agency had

---

[36]GAO-09-617.

established programs for implementing control categories, they also reported continuing weaknesses in those controls in the same year.

- One inspector general responded to the metric for plans of action and milestones (i.e., remediation program) that its agency had a remediation program in place that is consistent with FISMA requirements, tracks and monitors weaknesses, includes remediation plans that are effective at correcting weaknesses, remediates weaknesses in a timely manner, and adheres to milestone remediation dates. However, the inspector general audit of the agency's information security program identified 4,377 unremediated weaknesses, and the resulting report stated that component agencies were not entering or tracking all information security weaknesses.

- Another inspector general reported in response to the contractor systems metric that its agency updates the inventory of contractor systems at least annually; however, a report we issued on this agency's information security program identified a weakness in the accuracy of the agency's inventory of systems, including those systems operated by contractors. Specifically, the agency provided three different information systems inventories and none of them had the same information, reducing the agency's assurance that information systems were properly accounted for.

- In response to the configuration management metric, an inspector general at another agency stated that software scanning capabilities were fully implemented. However, the inspector general's independent evaluation showed that although the systems reviewed had the capability for software scanning, none of the systems were being fully scanned for vulnerabilities in accordance with agency requirements.

Without fully or consistently measuring the effectiveness of controls, DHS, OMB, and other stakeholders will lack insight into the performance of agencies' information security programs.

DHS Has Not Established Explicit Performance Targets for Many Metrics

In October 2011, we determined that of the 31 metrics for CIOs for fiscal year 2010, 30 of them did not include performance targets that would allow agencies to track progress over time.[37] We recommended that the Director of OMB incorporate performance targets for metrics in annual FISMA reporting guidance to agencies and inspectors general. OMB generally agreed with our recommendation.

In fiscal year 2012, DHS included explicit performance targets for metrics that were linked to the three cross-agency cybersecurity priority goals discussed earlier. For example, agencies were to ensure that 75 percent of all users were required to use personal identity verification cards to authenticate to their systems. While this partially addresses our previous recommendation, no explicit targets were established for metrics that did not relate to the three cross-agency cybersecurity priority goals, such as metrics related to data protection, incident management, configuration management, incident response and reporting, and remediation programs.

DHS officials acknowledged that these targets were needed, but that agency resources and the lack of DHS authority to establish targets have prevented the department from establishing additional targets. The officials also stated that only certain targets were included at this time in order to focus agency resources and senior leadership attention on those items that they believed would create the most change in federal information security. They added that additional targets will be included over time. Developing targets for additional metrics, as we previously recommended, will enable agencies and oversight entities to better gauge progress in securing federal systems.

DHS Inspector General Made Recommendations to Improve FISMA Oversight

In June 2013, the DHS inspector general issued a report on the results of its evaluation of whether DHS has implemented its additional cybersecurity responsibilities effectively to improve the security posture of the federal government.[38] It found that DHS had not developed a strategic

---

[37]GAO, *Information Security: Weaknesses Continue Amid New Federal Efforts to Implement Requirements,* GAO-12-137 (Washington, D.C.: Oct. 3, 2011).

[38]DHS OIG, *DHS Can Take Actions to Address Its Additional Cybersecurity Responsibilities,* OIG-13-95 (Washington, D.C.: June 5, 2013).

implementation plan that describes its cybersecurity responsibilities or establishes specific time frames and milestones to provide a clear plan of action for fulfilling those responsibilities. The report also stated that DHS had not established performance metrics to measure and monitor its progress in accomplishing its mission and goals. According to the inspector general, management turnover has hindered DHS's ability to develop a strategic implementation plan. Specifically, three key individuals essential to the DHS division overseeing FISMA compliance have left the agency since July 2012. The inspector general recommended that DHS coordinate with OMB to develop a strategic implementation plan that identifies long-term goals and milestones for federal agency FISMA compliance.

In addition, the inspector general found that some agencies indicated that DHS could make further improvements to the clarity and quality of the FISMA reporting metrics.[39] Specifically, five agencies indicated that some of the fiscal year 2012 and 2013 metrics were unclear and should be revised. In addition, two agencies stated that the reporting process was a strain on personnel resources because there are too many metrics. Some agency officials we interviewed echoed the need for clearer metrics and agreed that the process was time consuming. The inspector general recommended that DHS improve communication and coordination with federal agencies by providing additional clarity regarding the FISMA reporting metrics.

DHS agreed with the recommendations and officials stated that they are developing a strategic plan and documenting a methodology for metric development with the specific aim of improving the quality of the metrics, but did not state when the plan would be completed.

Inspectors General Conducted Independent Evaluations of Agency Information Security Programs

FISMA requires that agencies have an independent evaluation performed each year to evaluate the effectiveness of the agency's information security program and practices. FISMA also requires this evaluation to include (1) testing of the effectiveness of information security policies, procedures, and practices of a representative subset of the agency's information systems; and (2) an assessment of compliance with FISMA requirements, and related information security policies, procedures,

---

[39]The DHS inspector general interviewed 10 federal agencies: the Board of Governors of the Federal Reserve System; the Departments of Energy, Health and Human Services, Homeland Security, the Interior, Justice, State, and the Treasury; the Securities and Exchange Commission; and the Office of Personnel Management.

standards, and guidelines. For agencies with inspectors general, FISMA requires that these evaluations be performed by the inspector general or an independent external auditor. Lastly, FISMA requires that each year the agencies submit the results of these evaluations to OMB and that OMB summarize the results of the evaluations in its annual report to Congress. According to OMB, instructions for FISMA reporting, the metrics for inspectors general were designed to measure the effectiveness of agencies' information security programs and OMB relied on responses by inspectors general to gauge the effectiveness of information security program processes.

Our review of reports issued by inspectors general from the 24 major federal agencies in fiscal years 2011 and 2012 show that all 24 inspectors general conducted evaluations, identified weaknesses in agency information security programs and practices, and included recommendations to address the weaknesses. Inspectors general responded to the DHS-defined metrics for reporting on agency implementation of FISMA requirements, and most inspectors general also issued a more detailed audit report discussing the results of their evaluation of agency policies, procedures, and practices. One inspector general responded to the DHS metrics, but chose not to issue an additional detailed report on the results of the evaluation in fiscal year 2012. Three other inspectors general issued reports that summarized weaknesses contained in multiple reports throughout the reporting period.

NIST Continues to Provide Standards and Guidance to Assist Federal Agencies

To fulfill its responsibility to provide standards and guidance to agencies on information security, NIST has produced numerous information security standards and guidelines as well as updated existing information security publications. In April 2013, NIST released the fourth update of a key federal government computer security control guide, Special Publication 800-53: Security and Privacy Controls for Federal Information Systems and Organizations. According to NIST, the update was motivated by expanding threats and the increasing sophistication of cyber attacks. According to NIST, over 200 controls were added to help address these expanding threats and vulnerabilities. Examples include controls related to mobile and cloud computing; applications security; trustworthiness, assurance, and resiliency of information systems; insider threat; supply chain security; and the advanced persistent threat. As with previous versions of special publication 800-53, the controls contained in the latest update, according to NIST, can and should be tailored for specific needs of the agency and based on risk. In addition to this guide, NIST also issued and revised several other guidance documents. Table 7 lists recent NIST updates and releases.

Table 7: Recent NIST Updates and Releases

Publication number	Release date	Title
SP 800-124 Revision 1	June 2013	*Guidelines for Managing the Security of Mobile Devices in the Enterprise*
SP 800-56A Revision 2	May 2013	*Recommendation for Pair-Wise Key Establishment Schemes Using Discrete Logarithm Cryptography*
SP 800-53 Revision 4	April 2013	*Security and Privacy Controls for Federal Information Systems and Organizations*
SP 800-82 Revision 1	May 2013	*Guide to Industrial Control Systems (ICS) Security*
SP 800-30 Revision 1	September 2012	*Guide for Conducting Risk Assessments*
SP 800-61 Revision 2	August 2012	*Computer Security Incident Handling Guide*
SP 800-137	September 2011	*Information Security Continuous Monitoring (ISCM) for Federal Information Systems and Organizations*

Source: NIST.

In August 2012, NIST also published the National Cybersecurity Workforce Framework, which established a common taxonomy and lexicon that is to be used to describe all cybersecurity work and workers regardless of where or for whom the work is performed. This framework was developed as part of a larger effort to educate, recruit, train, develop, and retain a highly qualified workforce in the federal government as well as other sectors.

In addition, in partnership with the Department of Defense, the intelligence community, and the Committee on National Security Systems, NIST developed a unified information security framework to provide a common strategy to protect critical federal information systems and associated infrastructure for national security and non-national security systems. Historically, information systems in civilian agencies have operated under different security controls than military and intelligence systems. According to NIST, the framework provides standardized risk management policies, procedures, technologies, tools, and techniques that can be applied by all federal agencies. See table 8 for a list of publications that make up the framework.

Table 8: Unified Information Security Framework Publications

Publication number	Date	Title	Purpose
SP 800-53 Revision 4	April 2013	*Security and Privacy Controls for Federal Information Systems and Organizations*	To provide guidelines for selecting and specifying security controls for organizations and information systems supporting the executive agencies of the federal government to meet the requirements of Federal Information Processing Standards Publication 200, Minimum Security Requirements for Federal Information and Information Systems.
SP 800-30 Revision 1	September 2012	*Guide for Conducting Risk Assessments*	To provide guidance for conducting risk assessments of federal information systems and organizations, amplifying the guidance in Special Publication 800-39.
SP 800-39	March 2011	*Managing Information Security Risk: Organization, Mission, and Information System View*	To provide guidance for an integrated, organization-wide program for managing information security risk to organizational operations (i.e., mission, functions, image, and reputation), organizational assets, individuals, other organizations, and the nation resulting from the operation and use of federal information systems.
SP 800-53A Revision 1	June 2010[a]	*Guide for Assessing the Security Controls in Federal Information Systems and Organizations: Building Effective Security Assessment Plans*	To provide guidelines for building effective security assessment plans and a comprehensive set of procedures for assessing the effectiveness of security controls employed in information systems supporting the executive agencies of the federal government.
SP 800-37 Revision 1	February 2010	*Guide for Applying the Risk Management Framework to Federal Information Systems: A Security Life Cycle Approach*	To provide guidelines for applying the Risk Management Framework to federal information systems to include conducting the activities of security categorization, security control selection and implementation, security control assessment, information system authorization, and security control monitoring.

Source: NIST.

Conclusions

Although agencies have continued to make progress in implementing many of the requirements of FISMA, the remaining weaknesses continue to put federal information systems at risk of compromise. Specifically, agencies improved in implementing a program for managing information security risks; providing specialized training to employees and contractors; testing and evaluating systems on an annual basis; and detecting, responding to, and reporting security incidents. However,

[a]According to NIST officials, an update to SP 800-53A is expected to be released this year.

weaknesses continued to be identified for all of the components of an information security program, and we and agency inspectors general have made numerous recommendations to address these weaknesses and strengthen agencies' programs. These weaknesses show that information security continues to be a major challenge for federal agencies, and addressing these weaknesses is essential to establishing a robust security posture for the federal government. Until steps are taken to address these persistent challenges, overall progress in improving the nation's cybersecurity posture is likely to remain limited. Moreover, while OMB and DHS have continued to oversee agencies' FISMA implementation, they have not included all FISMA requirements; developed effectiveness measures; or, as we have recommended, established performance targets for many of the metrics agencies and inspectors general use to report on agencies' progress, making it more difficult to accurately assess the extent to which agencies are effectively securing their systems. Without more relevant metrics, OMB and DHS may lack adequate visibility into the federal government's information security posture.

Recommendations for Executive Action

We recommend that the Director of the Office of Management and Budget, in coordination with the Secretary of Homeland Security, take the following actions to enhance the usefulness of the annual FISMA reports and to provide additional insight into agencies' information security programs:

- develop compliance metrics related to periodic assessments of risk and development of subordinate security plans, and

- develop metrics for inspectors general to report on the effectiveness of agency information security programs.

Agency Comments and Our Evaluation

We provided a draft of this report to OMB, DHS, the Departments of Commerce, Education, Energy, and Transportation; the Environmental Protection Agency; and the Small Business Administration. The audit liaison for OMB responded via e-mail on September 10, 2013, that OMB generally agreed with our recommendations, but provided no other comments. In written comments provided by its Director of the Departmental GAO-Office of Inspector General Liaison Office (reproduced in appendix III), DHS concurred with both of our recommendations and identified actions it has taken or plans to take to implement our recommendations. For example, the department stated that it plans to work with OMB to include metrics specific to periodic assessments of risk and development of subordinate security plans, as well as to provide OMB with recommendations for metrics that inspectors general can use that focus on measuring the effectiveness of agency information security programs. According to DHS, these actions should be completed by the end of fiscal year 2014.

The audit liaison for NIST, within the Department of Commerce, provided technical comments via e-mail on September 4, 2013, and we incorporated them where appropriate. The audit liaisons for the Departments of Education, Energy, and Transportation; the Environmental Protection Agency; and the Small Business Administration responded via e-mail that the agencies did not have any comments.

We are sending copies of this report to the Director of the Office of Management and Budget, the Secretary of Homeland Security, and other interested parties. In addition, this report will be available at no charge on the GAO website at http://www.gao.gov.

If you have any questions regarding this report, please contact me at (202) 512-6244 or wilshuseng@gao.gov. Contact points for our Offices of Congressional Relations and Public Affairs may be found on the last page of this report. Key contributors to this report are listed in appendix III.

Gregory C. Wilshusen
Director, Information Security Issues

Appendix I: Objective, Scope, and Methodology

Our objective was to evaluate the extent to which the requirements of the Federal Information Security Management Act (FISMA) have been implemented, including the adequacy and effectiveness of agency information security policies and practices.

We reviewed and analyzed the provisions of the act to identify agency, Office of Management and Budget (OMB), and National Institute of Standards and Technology (NIST) responsibilities for implementing, overseeing, and providing guidance for agency information security to evaluate federal agencies' implementation of FISMA requirements. To assist in assessing the adequacy and effectiveness of agencies' information security policies and practices, we reviewed and analyzed FISMA data submissions and annual FISMA reports, as well as information security-related reports for each of the 24 major federal agencies based on work conducted in fiscal years 2011 and 2012 by us, agencies, and inspectors general. We reviewed and summarized weaknesses identified in those reports using FISMA requirements as well as the security control areas defined in our Federal Information System Controls Audit Manual.[1] Additionally, we analyzed, categorized, and summarized chief information officer and inspector general annual FISMA data submissions for fiscal years 2011 and 2012. Further, we compared weaknesses identified by inspectors general to the inspector general responses to the Department of Homeland Security (DHS)-defined metrics on the effectiveness of agency controls.

To assess the reliability of the agency-submitted data we obtained via CyberScope,[2] we reviewed supporting documentation that agencies provided to corroborate the data. We also conducted an assessment of the CyberScope application to gain an understanding of the data required, related internal controls, missing data, outliers, and obvious errors in submissions. We also reviewed a related DHS inspector general report that discussed its evaluation of the internal controls of CyberScope. In addition, we selected 6 agencies to gain an understanding of the quality of processes in place to produce annual FISMA reports. To select these agencies, we sorted the 24 major agencies from highest to lowest

---

[1]GAO, *Federal Information System Controls Audit Manual (FISCAM)*, GAO-09-232G (Washington, D.C.: February 2009).

[2]Cyberscope is an interactive data collection tool that has the capability to receive data feeds on a recurring basis to assess the security posture of a federal agency's information infrastructure. Agencies are required to use this tool to respond to reporting metrics.

using the total number of systems the agencies reported in fiscal year 2011; separated them into even categories of large, medium, and small agencies; then selected the median 2 agencies from each category.[3] These agencies were the Departments of Education, Energy, Homeland Security, and Transportation; the Environmental Protection Agency; and the Small Business Administration. We conducted interviews and collected data from the inspectors general and agency officials from the selected agencies to determine their process to ensure the reliability of data submissions. Based on this assessment, we determined that the data were sufficiently reliable for our work.

We also examined OMB and DHS FISMA reporting instructions and other guidance related to FISMA to determine the steps taken to evaluate the adequacy and effectiveness of agency information security programs. In addition, we interviewed officials from OMB, DHS's Federal Network Resilience Division, and NIST. We did not evaluate the implementation of DHS's FISMA-related responsibilities assigned to it by OMB.

We conducted this performance audit from February 2013 to September 2013 in accordance with generally accepted government auditing standards. Those standards require that we plan and perform the audit to obtain sufficient, appropriate evidence to provide a reasonable basis for our findings and conclusions based on our audit objectives. We believe that the evidence obtained provides a reasonable basis for our findings and conclusions based on our audit objectives.

---

[3]If the median agencies were selected in a previous year, another agency was selected. It is our intent to select all 24 major federal agencies within a 4-year report cycle.

Appendix II: Agency Responsibilities under FISMA

FISMA assigns a variety of responsibilities for federal information security to OMB, agencies, inspectors general, and NIST, which are described below.

Office of Management and Budget

FISMA states that the Director of the Office of Management and Budget (OMB) shall oversee agency information security policies and practices, including:

- developing and overseeing the implementation of policies, principles, standards, and guidelines on information security;

- requiring agencies to identify and provide information security protections commensurate with risk and magnitude of the harm resulting from the unauthorized access, use, disclosure, disruption, modification, or destruction of information collected or maintained by or on behalf of an agency, or information systems used or operated by an agency, or by a contractor of an agency, or other organization on behalf of an agency;

- overseeing agency compliance with FISMA; and

- reviewing at least annually and approving or disapproving, agency information security programs.

FISMA also requires OMB to report to Congress no later than March 1 of each year on agency compliance with the requirements of the act.

Federal Agencies

FISMA requires each agency, including agencies with national security systems, to develop, document, and implement an agency-wide information security program to provide security for the information and information systems that support the operations and assets of the agency, including those provided or managed by another agency, contractor, or other source.

Specifically, FISMA requires information security programs to include, among other things:

- periodic assessments of the risk and magnitude of harm that could result from the unauthorized access, use, disclosure, disruption, modification, or destruction of information or information systems;

- risk-based policies and procedures that cost-effectively reduce information security risks to an acceptable level and ensure that information security is addressed throughout the life cycle of each information system;

- subordinate plans for providing adequate information security for networks, facilities, and systems or groups of information systems, as appropriate;

- security awareness training for agency personnel, including contractors and other users of information systems that support the operations and assets of the agency;

- periodic testing and evaluation of the effectiveness of information security policies, procedures, and practices, performed with a frequency depending on risk, but no less than annually, and that includes testing of management, operational, and technical controls for every system identified in the agency's required inventory of major information systems;

- a process for planning, implementing, evaluating, and documenting remedial actions to address any deficiencies in the information security policies, procedures, and practices of the agency;

- procedures for detecting, reporting, and responding to security incidents; and

- plans and procedures to ensure continuity of operations for information systems that support the operations and assets of the agency.

In addition, agencies must produce an annually updated inventory of major information systems (including major national security systems) operated by the agency or under its control, which includes an identification of the interfaces between each system and all other systems or networks, including those not operated by or under the control of the agency.

FISMA also requires each agency to report annually to OMB, selected congressional committees, and the Comptroller General on the adequacy of its information security policies, procedures, practices, and compliance with requirements. In addition, agency heads are required to report annually the results of their independent evaluations to OMB, except to the extent that an evaluation pertains to a national security system; then only a summary and assessment of that portion of the evaluation needs to be reported to OMB.

Inspectors General

Under FISMA, the inspector general for each agency shall perform an independent annual evaluation of the agency's information security program and practices to determine the effectiveness of such program and practices. The evaluation should include testing of the effectiveness of information security policies, procedures, and practices of a representative subset of agency systems. In addition, the evaluation must include an assessment of the compliance with the act and any related information security policies, procedures, standards, and guidelines. For agencies without an inspector general, evaluations of non-national security systems must be performed by an independent external auditor. Evaluations related to national security systems are to be performed by an entity designated by the agency head.

National Institute of Standards and Technology

Under FISMA, the National Institute of Standards and Technology (NIST) is tasked with developing, for systems other than for national security, standards and guidelines that must include, at a minimum: (1) standards to be used by all agencies to categorize all their information and information systems based on the objectives of providing appropriate levels of information security according to a range of risk levels; (2) guidelines recommending the types of information and information systems to be included in each category; and (3) minimum information security requirements for information and information systems in each category. NIST must also develop a definition of and guidelines for detection and handling of information security incidents.

The law also assigns other information security functions to NIST including:

- providing technical assistance to agencies on elements such as compliance with the standards and guidelines, and the detection and handling of information security incidents;

- evaluating private-sector information security policies and practices and commercially available information technologies to assess potential application by agencies;

- evaluating security policies and practices developed for national security systems to assess their potential application by agencies; and
- conducting research, as needed, to determine the nature and extent of information security vulnerabilities and techniques for providing cost-effective information security.

In addition, FISMA requires NIST to prepare an annual report on activities undertaken during the previous year, and planned for the coming year, to carry out responsibilities under the act.

Appendix III: Comments from the Department of Homeland Security

U.S. Department of Homeland Security
Washington, DC 20528

Homeland Security

September 13, 2013

Gregory C. Wilshusen
Director, Information Security Issues
U.S. Government Accountability Office
441 G Street NW
Washington, DC 20548

Re: Draft Report GAO-13-776, "FEDERAL INFORMATION SECURITY: Mixed Progress
      in Implementing Program Components; Improved Metrics Needed to Measure
      Effectiveness"

Dear Mr. Wilshusen:

Thank you for the opportunity to review and comment on this draft report. The U.S. Department
of Homeland Security (DHS) appreciates the U.S. Government Accountability Office's (GAO's)
work in planning and conducting its review and issuing this report.

The Department is pleased to note GAO's positive recognition of the many efforts undertaken to
implement the requirements set forth in the Federal Information Security Management Act
(FISMA). These efforts include providing specialized training to employees and contractors,
implementing a risk management program, and testing/evaluating systems on an annual basis. In
addition, the report documents progress regarding the implementation of continuous monitoring
programs and also recognizes that most agencies have developed incident response and reporting
programs.

As a threshold matter, it is important to note that DHS suggests that the focus of federal
information security management should be on moving from the current compliance-based
metrics framework to one that establishes targets for acceptable security and measures
performance and outcomes as a part of Continuous Diagnostics and Mitigation (CDM). With the
advent of CDM, the focus will shift to security outcomes and prioritization of risks, whereas
under the current FISMA compliance framework, specific data as to the effectiveness of
mitigations and the true cost of non-compliance remain limited.

The legislative priority for CDM was codified in the Fiscal Year 2013 appropriations law,
allowing DHS's National Protection and Programs Directorate, Office of Cybersecurity and
Communications, Federal Network Resilience (FNR) Division to implement plans to compete
and award a Blanket Purchase Agreement (BPA) for Tools and Continuous Monitoring as a
Service. This law is also allowed for procuring a dashboard to provide scoring and prioritization
of risks. Leveraging available federal funding, FNR will deliver continuous diagnostics tools
and services to participating federal civilian agencies to be run on FNR's behalf. In addition, the

BPA is available to other government entities, including the Department of Defense, as well as state, local, tribal, and territorial governments.

The draft report contained two recommendations with which DHS concurs. Specifically, GAO recommended that the Director of the Office of Management and Budget (OMB), in coordination with the Secretary of Homeland Security:

Recommendation 1: Develop compliance metrics related to periodic assessment of risk and development of subordinate security plans.

Response: Concur. In March 2012, the White House Cybersecurity Coordinator announced that, in coordination with experts from DHS, the Department of Defense, the National Institute of Standards and Technology, and OMB, it had identified continuous monitoring of federal information systems as a priority area for improving federal cybersecurity. Over the coming months, FNR plans to meet regularly with OMB to discuss planning to address and closeout these actions. Accordingly, FNR has already reached out to OMB to begin gathering requirements specific to this recommendation as part of FNR support to achieve intended goals. FNR will provide OMB with recommendations for the expanded use of targets and metrics specific to periodic assessments of risk and development of subordinate security plans. Estimated Completion Date (ECD): December 31, 2013.

Recommendation 2: Develop metrics for inspectors general to report on the effectiveness of agency information security programs.

Response: Concur. FNR will provide OMB with recommendations for the metrics that Inspectors General can use and which focus on measuring the effectiveness of agency information security programs. ECD: September 30, 2014.

Again, thank you for the opportunity to review and provide comment on this draft report. Technical comments were previously provided under separate cover. Please feel free to contact me if you have any questions. We look forward to working with you in the future.

Sincerely,

Jim H. Crumpacker
Director
Departmental GAO-OIG Liaison Office

2

Appendix IV: GAO Contact and Staff Acknowledgments

GAO Contact	Gregory C. Wilshusen (202) 512-6244 or wilshuseng@gao.gov

Staff Acknowledgments	In addition to the individual named above, Anjalique Lawrence (assistant director), Cortland Bradford, Wil Holloway, Nicole Jarvis, Linda Kochersberger, Lee McCracken, Zsaroq Powe, David Plocher, Jena Sinkfield, Daniel Swartz, and Shaunyce Wallace made key contributions to this report.

GAO's Mission	The Government Accountability Office, the audit, evaluation, and investigative arm of Congress, exists to support Congress in meeting its constitutional responsibilities and to help improve the performance and accountability of the federal government for the American people. GAO examines the use of public funds; evaluates federal programs and policies; and provides analyses, recommendations, and other assistance to help Congress make informed oversight, policy, and funding decisions. GAO's commitment to good government is reflected in its core values of accountability, integrity, and reliability.
Obtaining Copies of GAO Reports and Testimony	The fastest and easiest way to obtain copies of GAO documents at no cost is through GAO's website (http://www.gao.gov). Each weekday afternoon, GAO posts on its website newly released reports, testimony, and correspondence. To have GAO e-mail you a list of newly posted products, go to http://www.gao.gov and select "E-mail Updates."
Order by Phone	The price of each GAO publication reflects GAO's actual cost of production and distribution and depends on the number of pages in the publication and whether the publication is printed in color or black and white. Pricing and ordering information is posted on GAO's website, http://www.gao.gov/ordering.htm.
	Place orders by calling (202) 512-6000, toll free (866) 801-7077, or TDD (202) 512-2537.
	Orders may be paid for using American Express, Discover Card, MasterCard, Visa, check, or money order. Call for additional information.
Connect with GAO	Connect with GAO on Facebook, Flickr, Twitter, and YouTube. Subscribe to our RSS Feeds or E-mail Updates. Listen to our Podcasts. Visit GAO on the web at www.gao.gov.
To Report Fraud, Waste, and Abuse in Federal Programs	Contact: Website: http://www.gao.gov/fraudnet/fraudnet.htm E-mail: fraudnet@gao.gov Automated answering system: (800) 424-5454 or (202) 512-7470
Congressional Relations	Katherine Siggerud, Managing Director, siggerudk@gao.gov, (202) 512-4400, U.S. Government Accountability Office, 441 G Street NW, Room 7125, Washington, DC 20548
Public Affairs	Chuck Young, Managing Director, youngc1@gao.gov, (202) 512-4800 U.S. Government Accountability Office, 441 G Street NW, Room 7149 Washington, DC 20548

Please Print on Recycled Paper.

www.ingramcontent.com/pod-product-compliance
Lightning Source LLC
Chambersburg PA
CBHW081707310526
45790CB00021B/2480